# What Does a Construction Worker Do?

## What Does a Community Helper Do?

P.M. Boekhoff

# Words to Know

architect (ARE-kuh-teckt)—A person who draws things for construction workers to build.

carpenter (CAR-pen-tur)—A person who builds with wood.

electrician (ee-leck-TRISH-un)—A person who puts in wires for electricity.

goggles (GAH-gulls)—Special glasses that protect the eyes.

joiner (JOY-nur)—A person who joins, or connects, wood to make windows and doors.

landscaper (LAND-skay-pur)—A person who plants gardens.

mason (MACE-n)—A person who builds with stone or brick.

plumber (PLUM-ur)—A person who puts in water pipes.

trowel (TRAU-uhl)—A tool used by a mason to put cement between bricks or stones.

## Enslow Elementary

an imprint of

## Enslow Publishers, Inc.

E

40 Industrial Road
Box 398
Berkeley Heights, NJ 07922
USA

PO Box 38
Aldershot
Hants GU12 6BP
UK

http://www.enslow.com

# Contents

**The architect draws plans that look like this.**

This architect shows the plans of a house to this couple.

# Build!

A new house will be built for a family. The architect has made the plans. He draws a floor plan and a picture of the house. He talks to the construction workers. He shows them where the house will be built.

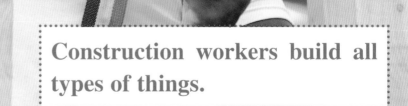

Construction workers build all types of things.

# Construction Workers Go To Work

Construction workers build houses. They also build ships, bridges, skyscrapers, and roads. They build with wood, metal, bricks, and stone. Some construction workers drive big machines.

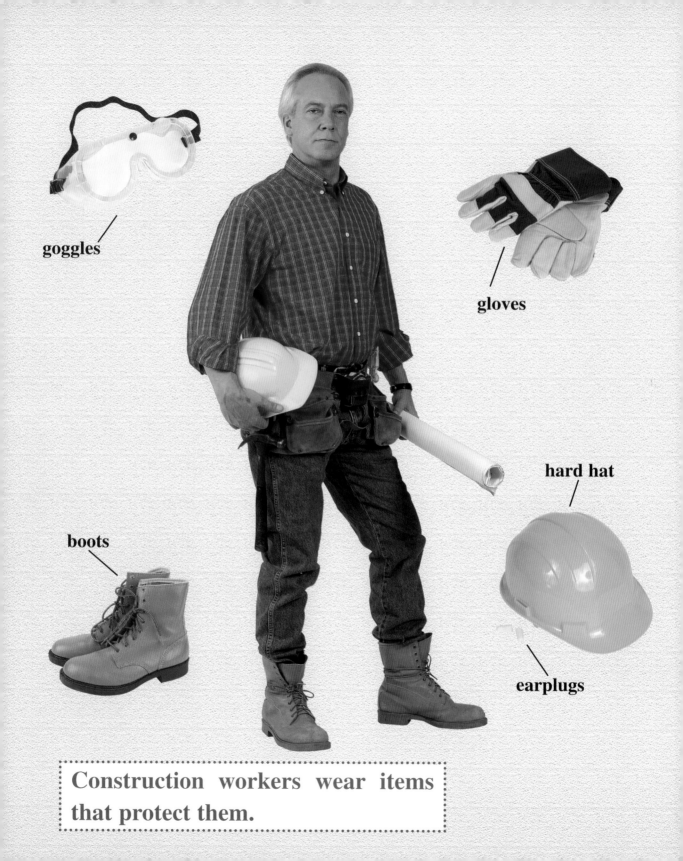

**goggles**

**gloves**

**boots**

**hard hat**

**earplugs**

Construction workers wear items that protect them.

# What Do Construction Workers Wear?

Construction workers wear special clothes to keep them safe. Hard hats protect their heads. Goggles protect their eyes. Heavy boots protect their feet. Gloves protect their hands. Earplugs protect their ears from the noise of the machines.

**Carpenters** build with wood.

# What Do Construction Workers Do?

Carpenters are construction workers who build with wood. They measure and cut the wood to match the architect's plans. They nail the wood together to make the house.

Roofers build the roof of the house.

**Masons** build the brick parts of a building. He is using a **trowel**.

Masons build with bricks and stones. Joiners join wood to make doors and windows. Roofers cover the house with a roof. Construction workers work together to build a house.

**Carpenter's tools**

**Plumber's tools**

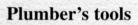

**Mason's tools**

**Electrician's tools**

# What Do Construction Workers Use?

Construction workers use special tools. Carpenters use hammers to nail wood together. Masons use trowels to put cement between bricks or stones to hold them together. Plumbers put water pipes in the house. Electricians use special tape to hold wires together.

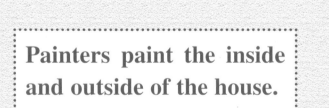

**Painters paint the inside and outside of the house.**

# The House Is Built

After the house is built, the workers keep working. Painters paint the house. Landscapers plant flowers and trees.

The new house is done! The family is ready to move in.

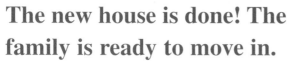

The construction workers clean all their tools and put them away. The house looks just like how the architect drew it. The happy family moves in.

Construction workers help out in their neighborhoods.

# Construction Workers Are Heroes

When their work is done, the construction workers go back to their own homes. They help their neighbors by fixing leaky roofs. They build playhouses for children. Construction workers are always ready to help.

# Be a Builder!

Would you like to be a builder? See if you can build a model of your bedroom. Ask an adult to help you.

*What You Will Need:*
- shoebox
- little boxes
- construction paper
- crayons or markers
- scissors
- glue or tape

1. The shoebox will be your room. If you want, cover the outside of the box in construction paper. Color the inside to match your room.

2. Look at your bedroom. Where is your bed? Where is your desk? Use the little boxes to show where everything is in your room. If you do not have little boxes, make the shapes out of construction paper.

3. Ask an adult to help you cut out a door and windows.

Now you have a small model of your room. How would you change it? Can you do the same with the other rooms in your home?

# Learn More

## Books

Anderson, Jenna. *How It Happens at the Building Site*. Minneapolis, Minn.: Clara House Books, 2004.

Hayward, Linda. *A Day in the Life of a Builder*. New York: Dorling Kindersley Pub., 2001.

Schaefer, Lola M. *Construction Site*. Chicago, Ill.: Heinemann Library, 2000.

## Internet Addresses

**B4UBuild.com Stuff 4 Kids**
<http://www.b4ubuild.com/kids/index.html>
This Web site includes stories, tools, projects, books, playhouses, and more. It has links to many Web sites about architecture, building and construction.

**Building Big**
<http://www.pbs.org/wgbh/buildingbig/>
Learn more about building big things—like bridges, skyscrapers, and dams.

# Index

**Note to Teachers and Parents:** The *What Does a Community Helper Do?* series supports curriculum standards for K–4 learning about community services and helpers. The Words to Know section introduces subject-specific vocabulary. Early readers may require help with these new words.

**Series Literacy Consultant:**
Allan A. De Fina, Ph.D.
Past President of the New Jersey Reading Association
Professor, Department of Literacy Education
New Jersey City University

Enslow Elementary, an imprint of Enslow Publishers, Inc.

Enslow Elementary® is a registered trademark
of Enslow Publishers, Inc.

**Library of Congress Cataloging-in-Publication Data**

Boekhoff, P. M. (Patti Marlene), 1957-
    What does a construction worker do? / P.M. Boekhoff.
        p. cm. — (What does a community helper do?)
    Includes bibliographical references and index.
    ISBN 0-7660-2326-5
    1. Building—Juvenile literature. 2. Architects and builders—Juvenile literature. 3. Contractors—Juvenile literature. I. Title. II. Series.
    TH149.B64 2006
    690'.023—dc22
                                    2005017579

Printed in the United States of America

10 9 8 7 6 5 4 3 2 1

**To Our Readers:**
We have done our best to make sure all Internet Addresses in this book were active and appropriate when we went to press. However, the author and the publisher have no control over and assume no liability for the material available on those Internet sites or on other Web sites they may link to. Any comments or suggestions can be sent by e-mail to comments@enslow.com or to the address on the back cover.

**Illustration Credits:** brand X pictures, pp. 4 (bottom), 6 (background), 16 (top), 18 (all), 20; Hemera Technologies, Inc. 1997–2000, pp. 2, 13, 19; © 2005 JupiterImages, pp. 1, 4 (top), 6 (inset), 8 (all), 10, 12 (all), 14 (all), 16 (bottom), 22.

**Cover Illustration:** © 2005 JupiterImages (bottom); top left to right (brand X pictures, first two; © 2005 JupiterImages, last two).